This B✦✦k
Belongs To:

_____

Thank you for choosing this book! I hope you found it not only entertaining for your child, but also a great way for them to learn more about the Bible through fun activities. Please don't forget to leave a review on Amazon! Your input is always appreciated and valued!

The QR code below takes you to the Journey in Grace author page where you can see what other books are offered. It will also give you links to find them on Amazon.

Why Do We Need Jesus?

IT ALL GOES BACK TO ADAM AND EVE EATING FRUIT FROM
THE TREE GOD TOLD THEM NOT TO.

God said, ..."Have you eaten from the tree that I commanded you not
to eat from?
The man said, "The woman whom you gave to be with me, she gave
me the fruit from the tree, and I ate it."
Yahweh God said to the woman, "What have you done?"
The woman said, "The serpent deceived me, and I ate...."

Genesis 3:11-13 WEB

Therefore, as sin entered into the world through one man (Adam),
and death through sin, so death passed to all men because all sinned.

Romans 5:12 WEB

BUT GOD MADE A PROMISE THAT GAVE A GLIMPSE OF THE
PLAN HE HAD TO SAVE US FROM SIN AND DEATH.

"I will put hostility between you and the woman, and between your
offspring and her offspring.
He will bruise your head,
and you will bruise his heel."

Genesis 3:15 WEB

Adam and Eve's Sin

Color the Picture

Spot the Difference
Spot 6 Differences Below and Circle Them

Adam and Eve's Sin
Find the Path to the Forbidden Tree

THIS WAY

Adam and Eve's Sin

```
D  W  H  N  V  H  Z  S  Z  D  V  A  E  T
E  V  R  S  W  E  L  W  B  H  K  E  W  Q
C  D  E  D  N  A  M  M  O  C  X  G  J  U
E  P  I  W  C  D  J  S  M  A  N  L  J  N
I  F  W  N  X  G  T  I  B  D  E  Y  O  F
V  G  B  R  U  I  S  E  E  E  A  O  N  Z
E  S  N  S  L  A  Z  Z  H  H  T  E  W  O
D  P  F  I  E  F  O  T  R  E  E  E  O  I
F  O  T  X  R  R  S  T  A  W  N  S  M  V
Q  Y  K  U  Z  P  P  M  T  H  Z  A  V
R  Q  I  P  G  F  S  E  F  A  U  M  N  R
K  T  E  W  H  L  B  F  N  Y  S  G  L  K
Y  K  A  Y  M  G  M  N  F  T  P  V  L  K
B  N  S  S  Y  R  Y  G  H  O  B  T  K  J
```

YAHWEH	MAN	WOMAN
SERPENT	EATEN	COMMANDED
TREE	FRUIT	DECEIVED
HOSTILITY	BETWEEN	OFFSPRING
BRUISE	HEAD	HEEL

Adam and Eve's Sin

Use the passage for Adam and Eve's Sin to solve the crossword

Across:

1. God said, Have you _____ from the tree? Gen 3:11"

2. Who the hostility will be between. Gen 3:15

3. What Eve's offspring will do to the serpent's head. Gen 3:15

4. What the serpent will bruise on Eve's offspring. Gen 3:15

Down:

5. What God will put between the serpent and the woman. Gen 3:15

6. Who Eve's offspring refers to...think Bethlehem. Gen 3:15

7. Who Adam blamed. Gen 3:12

8. Who Eve blamed. Gen 3:13

9. This was on the tree. Gen 3:12

10. What the serpent did to get Eve to eat the fruit. Gen 3:13

Adam and Eve's Sin
Word Scramble

Use the passage for Adam and Eve's sin to unscramble these words

TNAEE = _____

EMACMDDNO = _____

UITFR = _____

TPNESER = _____

YHILTOSTI = _____

EETR = _____

WMAON = _____

ETA = _____

VCEEDEID = _____

RIUBSE = _____

Adam and Eve's Sin

Hint: Whose head will be bruised?

God's Solution to Sin Shown to Abraham

1Now Yahweh said to Abram, "Leave your country, and your relatives, and your father's house, and go to the land that I will show you.
2 I will make of you a great nation. I will bless you and make your name great. You will be a blessing.
3 I will bless those who bless you, and I will curse him who treats you with contempt. All the families of the earth will be blessed through you."

Genesis 12:1-3 WEB

5 Yahweh brought him outside, and said, "Look now toward the sky, and count the stars, if you are able to count them." He said to Abram, "So your offspring will be." 6 He believed in Yahweh, who credited it to him for righteousness.

Genesis 15:5-6 WEB

HOW WOULD ALL THE FAMILIES OF THE EARTH
BE BLESSED THROUGH ABRAHAM? THINK BETHLEHEM!

God's Promise to Abraham

Color the Picture

Spot the Difference
Spot 6 Differences Below and Circle Them

God's Promise to Abraham

Find Abraham's path to the Promised Land

God's Promise to Abraham

```
P  L  H  L  I  U  V  E  K  J  L  Z  J  T
Q  U  S  Q  A  W  B  E  Z  M  I  W  A  A
Z  C  S  G  R  F  I  B  H  I  L  F  V  H
E  Z  S  N  O  I  T  A  N  W  G  V  R  C
X  D  S  E  F  W  P  L  T  U  I  P  R  Z
E  C  S  L  V  B  M  S  A  M  Y  Y  B  B
F  Q  E  Z  Y  I  E  A  E  O  K  Q  V  H
S  A  L  D  B  I  T  P  R  O  H  T  E  V
L  H  B  E  L  V  N  A  G  B  V  V  V  W
U  T  N  I  E  E  O  E  L  O  A  O  E  H
L  R  M  I  V  U  C  A  R  E  X  S  C  J
R  A  Q  P  X  K  N  R  L  E  R  L  M  S
F  E  L  A  Y  D  O  Z  G  U  U  J  D  Q
Y  H  B  L  B  I  I  C  C  S  A  J  U  O
```

ABRAM	LEAVE	RELATIVES
LAND	GREAT	NATION
BLESS	CURSE	CONTEMPT
ALL	FAMILIES	EARTH

God's Promise to Abraham

Use the passage for God's Promise to Abraham to solve the crossword

Across:

1. Abraham's first name. Gen 12:1

2. What God told Abram to do. Gen 12:1

3. Third thing Abram was to leave. Gen 12:1

4. Abram would be made a great _____. Gen 12:2

5. God will do this to those who treat with contempt. Gen 12:3

Down:

6. First thing Abram was to leave. Gen 12:1

7. Second thing Abram was to leave. Gen 12:1

8. God will make Abram's name _____. Gen 12:2

9. Abram will be this. Gen 12:2

10. Who will be blessed through Abram. Gen 12:3

God's Promise to Abraham
Word Scramble

Use the passage for God's Promise to Abraham to unscramble these words

BARAM   = _____

EAEILSVRT   = _____

AGTER   = _____

LSSBE   = _____

IFLIASME   = _____

AELEV   = _____

DLNA   = _____

ONNTAI   = _____

SCEUR   = _____

ATRHE   = _____

SECRET CODE

USE THE DECODER MAP BELOW
TO DECODE THE SECRET MESSAGE

1 12 12   20 8 5   6 1 13 9 12 9 5 19   15 6

20 8 5   5 1 18 20 8   23 5 18 5

2 12 5 19 19 5 4   20 8 18 15 21 7 8

1 2 18 1 8 1 13   23 8 5 14   10 5 19 21 19

3 1 13 5

DECODER MAP

1=A	2=B	3=C	4=D	5=E	6=F
7=G	8=H	9=I	10=J	11=K
12=L	13=M	14=N	15=O	16=P
17=Q	18=R	19=S	20=T	21=U
22=V	23=W	24=X	25=Y	26=Z

The Angel Tells Mary Jesus Will Be Born To Her

26 Now in the sixth month, the angel Gabriel was sent from God to a city of Galilee named Nazareth,

27 to a virgin pledged to be married to a man whose name was Joseph, of David's house. The virgin's name was Mary.

28 Having come in, the angel said to her, "Rejoice, you highly favored one! The Lord is with you. Blessed are you among women."

29 But when she saw him, she was greatly troubled at the saying...

30 The angel said to her, "Don't be afraid, Mary, for you have found favor with God.

31 Behold, you will conceive in your womb and give birth to a son, and shall name him 'Jesus.'

34 Mary said to the angel, "How can this be...?"

35 The angel answered her, "The Holy Spirit will come on you, and the power of the Most High will overshadow you.

38 Mary said, "Behold, the servant of the Lord; let it be done to me according to your word."

Luke 1:26-31, 34-35, 38 WEB

The Angel Tells Mary Jesus Will Be Born To Her

Color the Picture

Spot the Difference
Spot 6 Differences Below and Circle Them

The Angel Tells Mary Jesus Will Be Born To Her

Help the angel find Mary

The Angel Tells Mary Jesus Will Be Born To Her

```
Y  F  A  K  S  U  L  P  W  P  L  M  M
P  G  S  S  A  L  V  J  D  T  F  F  W
U  A  A  W  N  D  X  W  Y  R  A  M  N
N  B  O  F  G  V  E  O  Q  M  S  S  O
L  R  A  S  E  E  I  R  K  X  E  K  B
D  I  J  D  L  L  R  R  O  J  R  R  S
F  E  O  I  E  D  B  I  G  V  V  I  H
P  L  L  Q  L  S  F  K  T  I  A  A  P
E  A  A  B  J  E  S  U  S  Z  N  F  E
G  F  L  G  U  M  S  E  A  O  T  Y  S
F  O  Z  I  S  O  Z  H  L  V  S  J  O
E  M  X  D  J  T  R  F  X  B  X  W  J
A  N  A  Z  A  R  E  T  H  T  N  O  M
```

MONTH	GABRIEL	GALILEE
NAZARETH	VIRGIN	JOSEPH
MARY	ANGEL	FAVORED
BLESSED	TROUBLED	JESUS
SERVANT	WORD	

The Angel Tells Mary Jesus Will Be Born To Her

Use the passage for The Angel Tells Mary to solve the crossword

ACROSS:

1. THE MONTH THE ANGEL CAME TO MARY. LUKE 1:26

2. NAME OF THE ANGEL. LUKE 1:26

3. REJOICE, YOU HIGHLY _____ ONE. LUKE 1:28

4. THE NAME MARY WOULD GIVE TO HER SON. LUKE 1:31

5. THE _____ SPIRIT WOULD OVERSHADOW MARY. LUKE 1:35

6. LET IT BE DONE ACCORDING TO GOD'S _____. LUKE 1:38

DOWN:

7. THE CITY WHERE MARY LIVED. LUKE 1:26

8. THE MAN MARY WAS PLEDGED TO BE MARRIED TO. LUKE 1:27

9. WHAT MARY WAS WHEN THE ANGEL GREETED HER. LUKE 1:29

10. MARY WOULD GIVE _____ TO A SON. LUKE 1:31

11. MARY DESCRIBES HERSELF AS THIS. LUKE 1:38

The Angel Tells Mary Jesus Will Be Born To Her Word Scramble

Use the passage for The Angel Tells Mary to unscramble these words

XHIST = _____

IEGLELA = _____

RIDAMER = _____

CEOJREI = _____

ETLORDBU = _____

MNTHO = _____

NIVGRI = _____

ENLAG = _____

EFDRVAO = _____

NRSTVEA = _____

Color By Number

Use the color map below to color the picture

5	5	5	5	5	5	5	5	5	5	5	5	5	5	5	5	5	5	5	5	5	5	5	5	5	5	5	5	5	5	5	5
5	5	5	5	5	5	5	5	5	5	5	5	5	5	5	5	5	5	5	5	5	5	5	5	5	5	5	5	5	5	5	5
5	5	5	5	5	1	5	5	5	5	5	5	5	5	5	5	5	5	5	5	5	5	5	5	5	1	5	5	5	5	5	
5	5	5	5	1	1	5	5	5	5	5	5	5	5	5	5	5	5	5	5	5	5	5	5	1	1	5	5	5	5		
5	5	5	5	1	1	1	5	5	5	5	5	5	5	5	5	5	5	5	5	5	5	1	1	1	5	5	5	5			
5	5	5	1	1	1	1	1	5	5	5	5	5	5	5	5	5	5	5	5	5	1	1	1	1	1	5	5	5			
5	5	5	1	1	1	1	1	1	5	5	5	5	5	5	5	5	5	5	5	1	1	1	1	1	1	5	5	5			
5	5	5	1	1	1	1	1	1	1	5	5	2	2	2	5	5	1	1	1	1	1	1	1	1	5	5	5				
5	5	5	1	1	1	1	1	1	1	5	2	2	2	2	2	5	5	1	1	1	1	1	1	1	5	5	5				
5	5	5	5	1	1	1	1	1	1	1	5	2	2	2	2	2	5	1	1	1	1	1	1	1	5	5	5	5			
5	5	5	5	1	1	1	1	1	1	1	5	2	2	2	2	2	5	1	1	1	1	1	1	1	5	5	5	5			
5	5	5	5	1	1	1	1	1	1	1	5	2	2	2	5	5	1	1	1	1	1	1	1	5	5	5	5				
5	5	5	5	5	1	1	1	1	1	1	5	3	3	3	5	5	1	1	1	1	1	1	5	5	5	5	5				
5	5	5	5	5	1	1	1	1	1	1	3	3	3	3	3	1	1	1	1	1	1	5	5	5	5	5	5				
5	5	5	5	5	5	1	1	1	1	1	3	3	3	3	3	1	1	1	1	1	5	5	5	5	5	5	5				
5	5	5	5	5	5	5	1	1	1	1	3	3	3	3	3	1	1	1	5	5	5	5	5	5	5	5	5				
5	5	5	5	5	5	5	5	5	5	5	3	3	3	3	3	3	5	5	5	5	5	5	5	5	5	5	5				
5	5	5	5	5	5	5	5	5	5	5	3	3	3	3	3	3	5	5	5	5	5	5	5	5	5	5	5				
5	5	5	5	5	5	5	5	5	5	5	3	3	3	3	3	3	5	5	5	5	5	5	5	5	5	5	5				
5	5	5	5	5	5	5	5	5	5	5	3	3	3	3	3	3	5	5	5	5	5	5	5	5	5	5	5				
5	5	5	5	5	5	5	5	5	5	5	3	3	3	3	3	3	5	5	5	5	5	5	5	5	5	5	5				
5	5	5	5	5	5	5	5	5	5	3	3	3	4	4	4	3	3	3	5	5	5	5	5	5	5	5	5				
5	5	5	5	5	5	5	5	5	3	3	3	3	4	4	4	3	3	3	5	5	5	5	5	5	5	5	5				
5	5	5	5	5	5	5	5	3	3	3	3	4	4	4	4	4	3	3	3	5	5	5	5	5	5	5	5				
5	5	5	5	5	5	5	3	3	3	3	3	4	4	4	4	4	3	3	3	3	5	5	5	5	5	5	5				
5	5	5	5	5	5	5	3	3	3	3	3	4	4	4	4	4	3	3	3	3	3	5	5	5	5	5	5				
5	5	5	5	5	5	5	3	3	3	3	4	4	4	4	4	4	3	3	3	3	5	5	5	5	5	5	5				
5	5	5	5	5	5	5	3	3	3	4	4	4	4	4	4	4	4	3	3	5	5	5	5	5	5	5	5				
5	5	5	5	5	5	5	5	5	5	5	5	5	4	4	4	4	4	5	5	5	5	5	5	5	5	5	5				
5	5	5	5	5	5	5	5	5	5	5	5	5	5	5	5	5	5	5	5	5	5	5	5	5	5	5	5				
5	5	5	5	5	5	5	5	5	5	5	5	5	5	5	5	5	5	5	5	5	5	5	5	5	5	5	5				

Color Map

1 = yellow   2 = pink   3 = light blue

4 = dark blue   5 = green

NO ROOM!

1 Now in those days, a decree went out from Caesar Augustus that all the world should be enrolled

2 This was the first enrollment made when Quirinius was governor of Syria.

3 All went to enroll themselves, everyone to his own city.

4 Joseph also went up from Galilee, out of the city of Nazareth, into Judea, to David's city, which is called Bethlehem, because he was of the house and family of David

5 to enroll himself with Mary, who was pledged to be married to him as wife, being pregnant.

6 While they were there, the day had come for her to give birth.

7 She gave birth to her firstborn son. She wrapped him in bands of cloth and laid him in a feeding trough, because there was no room for them in the inn.

Luke 2:1-7 WEB

NO ROOM!
Color the Picture

Spot the Difference
Spot 6 Differences Below and Circle Them

NO ROOM!
Help Mary and Joseph find the stable

NO ROOM!

```
G  G  O  I  S  P  C  H  X  S  X  Z  Y  W
T  H  T  R  O  U  G  H  U  K  Z  V  L  O
Z  B  F  A  O  M  I  N  N  K  G  Y  P  U
A  E  I  F  L  N  V  N  R  J  S  P  I  R
D  T  Q  X  G  B  A  V  I  A  O  J  F  K
U  H  R  R  I  G  J  Z  R  R  S  P  X  Y
P  L  W  R  K  V  A  F  A  C  I  E  X  T
N  E  T  P  W  V  Q  L  Q  R  N  U  A  I
V  H  J  O  R  J  M  F  I  R  E  B  Q  C
S  E  P  O  A  W  M  B  O  L  A  T  Z  L
O  M  O  Z  P  E  L  L  M  G  E  T  H  O
V  M  F  M  P  T  L  E  E  R  C  E  D  T
W  M  H  R  E  E  M  Z  I  L  E  Z  R  H
Q  Q  E  G  D  X  S  I  W  W  P  C  C  S
```

DECREE	CAESAR	ENROLLED
QUIRINIUS	CITY	GALILEE
NAZARETH	BETHLEHEM	BIRTH
WRAPPED	CLOTHS	TROUGH
ROOM	INN	

NO ROOM!

Use the passage for NO ROOM! to solve the crossword

Across:

1. Everyone went to his own _____ to enroll. Luke 2:3

2. Where David went to enroll. Luke 2:4

3. Joseph was of the family of this person. Luke 2:4

4. What Mary did with Jesus. Luke 2:7

5. Where Mary laid Jesus. Luke 2:6

Down:

6. What went out from Caesar. Luke 2:1

7. All of this should be enrolled. Luke 2:1

8. Who was governor of Syria. Luke 2:2

9. Mary's condition at this time. Luke 2:5

10. Jesus was Mary's _____ son. Luke 2:6

NO ROOM!
Word Scramble
Use the passage for NO ROOM! to unscramble these words

CDREEE = _____

HMBEELTHE = _____

IRHBT = _____

APPDRWE = _____

HUOGRT = _____

DORLELEN = _____

NGPENRAT = _____

NFTRSBIRO = _____

TLHCO = _____

RMOO = _____

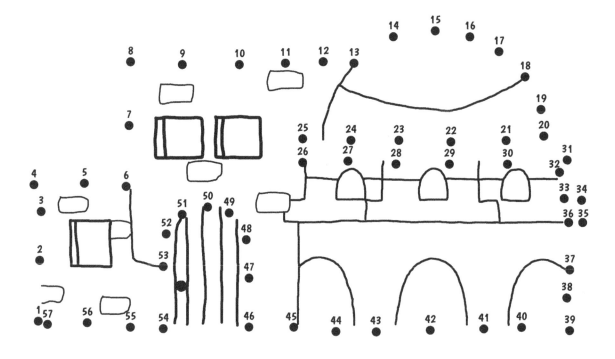

in Bethlehem

The Angel Tells Shepherds About Jesus' Birth

8 There were shepherds in the same country staying in the field, and keeping watch by night over their flock. 9 Behold, an angel of the Lord stood by them, and the glory of the Lord shone around them, and they were terrified. 10 The angel said to them, "Don't be afraid, for behold, I bring you good news of great joy which will be to all the people. 11 For there is born to you today, in David's city, a Savior, who is Christ the Lord.
12 This is the sign to you; you will find a baby wrapped in strips of cloth, lying in a feeding trough." 13 Suddenly, there was with the angel a multitude of the heavenly army praising God and saying,

14 "Glory to God in the highest,

on earth peace, good will toward men."

15 When the angels went away from them into the sky, the shepherds said to one another, "Let's go to Bethlehem, now, and see this thing that has happened, which the Lord has made known to us." 16 They came with haste and found both Mary and Joseph, and the baby was lying in the feeding trough....20 The shepherds returned, glorifying and praising God for all the things that they had heard and seen, just as it was told them.
Luke 2:8-16, 20 WEB

The Angel Tells Shepherds About Jesus' Birth

Color the Picture

Spot the Difference
Spot 6 Differences Below and Circle Them

The Angel Tells Shepherds About Jesus' Birth
Help the Angel Find the Shepherds

The Angel Tells Shepherds About Jesus' Birth

```
P  F  R  D  Q  I  D  B  U  I  E  X  N  J
D  V  E  V  K  P  P  I  X  Y  C  K  R  B
Q  I  B  R  O  I  V  A  S  B  A  B  Y  N
Y  X  A  J  L  D  A  K  P  M  E  B  M  A
H  P  H  R  U  Z  X  V  Y  K  P  X  R  J
S  T  S  H  F  N  G  I  S  S  C  L  A  Q
Y  D  E  P  P  A  R  W  G  T  S  O  Q  Y
R  R  K  R  G  S  J  K  W  W  Q  V  L  D
V  Z  O  Y  R  C  N  U  C  T  N  N  T  F
H  J  O  L  F  I  E  L  D  L  E  G  N  A
A  J  T  U  G  N  F  R  U  V  O  O  F  T
K  D  R  H  E  J  R  I  A  U  T  O  X  B
K  U  T  W  Y  D  N  E  E  U  K  D  B  I
E  M  S  H  E  P  H  E  R  D  S  X  D  N
```

SHEPHERDS	FIELD	FLOCK
NIGHT	ANGEL	GLORY
TERRIFIED	AFRAID	GOOD
NEWS	JOY	SAVIOR
SIGN	BABY	WRAPPED
HEAVENLY	ARMY	PEACE

The Angel Tells Shepherds About Jesus' Birth

Use the passage for The Angel Tells Shepherds to solve the crossword

Across:

1. The angel told them not to be _____. Luke 2:10

2. What kind of news did the angel bring? Luke 2:10

3. Who was born unto them that day? Luke 2:11

4. This is a _____ to you. Luke 2:12

5. The baby would be wrapped in strips of _____. Luke 2:12

6. Glory to God and on earth _____. Luke 2:14

Down:

1. Who came to see the shepherds. Luke 2:9

7. Who was in a field. Luke 2:8

8. What the shepherds were watching over. Luke 2:8

9. The _____ of the Lord shone around them. Luke 2:9

10. How the shepherds felt when they saw the angel. Luke 2:9

11. The news was of great _____. Luke 2:10

The Angel Tells Shepherds About Jesus' Birth Word Scramble

Use the passage for The Angel Tells Shepherds to unscramble these words

EEHSRPDHS = _____

WCHTA = _____

GRLOY = _____

SWNE = _____

SNIG = _____

DLFEI = _____

COLKF = _____

DEEIRTIRF = _____

JYO = _____

LTTIMUDUE = _____

Where's the Sheep?

Find the one sheep that has a different eye

Find the one sheep that has a different mouth

Find the one sheep that has a different nose

Find the shepherd

Jesus is Born

18 Now the birth of Jesus Christ was like this: After his mother, Mary, was engaged to Joseph, before they came together, she was found pregnant by the Holy Spirit.

19 Joseph, her husband, being a righteous man, and not willing to make her a public example, intended to put her away secretly.

20 But when he thought about these things, behold, an angel of the Lord appeared to him in a dream saying, "Joseph, son of David, don't be afraid to take to yourself Mary as your wife, for that which is conceived in her is of the Holy Spirit.

21 She shall give birth to a son. You shall name him Jesus, for it is he who shall save his people from their sins."

22 Now all this happened that it might be fulfilled which was spoken by the Lord through the prophet, saying,

Behold, the virgin shall be with child,

and shall give birth to a son.

They shall call his name Immanuel." which is, being interpreted,

"God with us."

Matthew 1:18-23 WEB

Jesus is Born
Color the Picture

Spot the Difference
Spot 6 Differences Below and Circle Them

Jesus is Born
Help the Shepherds Find Jesus

Jesus is Born

```
Z  H  B  S  J  J  Z  K  V  Z  G  W  S  J
V  T  X  E  P  O  F  R  H  X  E  Y  B  I
E  L  R  D  B  S  U  T  Y  V  N  C  M  W
J  J  Y  I  J  E  D  N  S  R  G  M  M  W
P  T  V  E  G  P  C  A  F  R  A  I  D  P
H  L  S  S  S  H  V  N  D  N  G  M  S  W
B  U  Y  D  O  E  T  G  U  Y  E  A  C  V
S  E  K  N  N  T  C  E  S  B  D  W  Q  C
T  N  O  R  H  A  L  R  O  P  U  G  D  Y
G  Z  I  F  U  N  F  P  E  U  W  T  R  X
Q  X  J  S  T  G  J  D  A  T  S  X  R  K
A  N  G  O  M  E  X  A  M  P  L  E  G  C
U  Q  A  V  A  L  S  I  V  T  K  Y  H  U
Z  I  V  I  B  B  I  R  T  H  V  O  F  I
```

ENGAGED	PREGNANT	MARY
JOSEPH	RIGHTEOUS	EXAMPLE
SECRETLY	ANGEL	AFRAID
BIRTH	SON	JESUS
SAVE	SINS	IMMANUEL

Jesus is Born
Use the passage for Jesus is Born to solve the crossword

ACROSS:

1. MARY WAS _____ TO JOSEPH. MATT 1:18

2. JOSEPH DIDN'T WANT TO MAKE MARY A PUBLIC _____. MATT 1:19

3. THE ANGEL APPEARED TO JOSEPH IN A _____. MATT 1:20

4. WHAT JESUS WOULD DO FOR HIS PEOPLE. MATT 1:21

5. ALL THIS HAPPENED SO THAT IT MIGHT BE _____. MATT 1:22

6. IMMANUEL MEANS GOD _____ US. MATT 1:23

DOWN:

7. MARY'S HUSBAND. MATT 1:19

8. THE KIND OF MAN JOSEPH WAS. MATT 1:19

9. HOW JOSEPH WAS GOING TO PUT MARY AWAY. MATT 1:19

10. WHO CAME TO JOSEPH. MATT 1:20

11. THE ANGEL TOLD JOSEPH NOT TO BE _____. MATT 1:20

12. WHO DID THE LORD SPEAK A PROPHECY THROUGH. MATT 1:22

13. THEY SHALL CALL HIS NAME _____. MATT 1:23

Jesus is Born
Word Scramble
Use the passage for Jesus is Born to unscramble these words

AYMR = _____

SUDHNAB = _____

LPIUBC = _____

ETLECSYR = _____

AVES = _____

HPJOSE = _____

RGHOETUSI = _____

LEXMAEP = _____

DAMER = _____

DAEPDETR = _____

Use a white crayon or colored pencil to do the dot-to dot and then color the background

Wise Men See the Star

1 Now when Jesus was born in Bethlehem of Judea in the days of King Herod, behold, wise men from the east came to Jerusalem, saying,

2 "Where is he who is born King of the Jews? For we saw his star in the east, and have come to worship him."

3 When King Herod heard it, he was troubled, and all Jerusalem with him.

4 Gathering together all the chief priests and scribes of the people, he asked them where the Christ would be born...

7 Then Herod secretly called the wise men, and learned from them exactly what time the star appeared.

8 He sent them to Bethlehem, and said, "Go and search diligently for the young child. When you have found him, bring me word, so that I also may come and worship him."

9...and behold, the star, which they (the wise men) saw in the east, went before them until it came and stood over where the young child was.

10 When they saw the star, they rejoiced with exceedingly great joy.

Matthew 2:1-4, 7-10 WEB

Wise Men See the Star
Color the Picture

Spot the Difference
Spot 6 Differences Below and Circle Them

Wise Men See the Star
Help the Wise Men Follow the Star

Wise Men See the Star

```
R  E  B  E  T  H  L  E  H  E  M  V  N  R
L  A  Y  O  J  X  C  D  H  B  W  C  S  K
K  A  T  J  N  H  M  O  U  U  B  Z  B  S
O  W  I  S  E  M  E  N  B  H  D  E  A  T
Z  M  S  Q  H  S  L  R  C  E  A  Y  L  S
Y  X  B  Q  M  R  A  O  L  R  W  O  M  I
U  L  K  X  M  E  S  B  S  O  O  H  C  B
H  N  T  Q  J  J  U  H  J  D  R  N  R  F
K  V  T  E  O  O  R  K  N  W  S  G  L  C
O  P  S  S  R  I  E  X  V  C  H  S  X  V
Q  D  A  T  E  C  J  T  R  U  I  L  Q  H
L  H  E  Q  Y  E  E  Z  X  I  P  T  A  F
V  S  T  O  O  D  I  S  V  K  W  I  N  D
S  L  T  D  L  N  M  M  M  I  O  H  V  M
```

HEROD	WISEMEN	EAST
STAR	WORSHIP	TROUBLED
JERUSALEM	BORN	BETHLEHEM
SECRETLY	STOOD	REJOICED
JOY		

Wise Men See the Star

Use the passage for Wise Men See the Star to solve the crossword

Across:

1. Who was king when Jesus was born. Matt 2:1

2. These came from the east. Matt 2:1

3. Jesus was considered the _____ of the Jews. Matt 2:2

4. How Herod called the wise men. Matt 2:7

5. What Herod said he would do when they found Jesus. Matt 2:8

Down:

6. Where Jesus was born. Matt. 2:1

7. This was seen in the east. Matt 2:2

8. King Herod was _____ when he heard it. Matt 2:3

9. Go and search _____ for the young child. Matt 2:8

10. What the wisemen did when they saw the star. Matt 2:10

Wise Men See the Star
Word Scramble
Use the passage for Wise Men See the Star to unscramble these words

SEMNEIW = _____

KNGI = _____

OERBDTLU = _____

JCIEODRE = _____

EYRCLTSE = _____

RLSJEEAUM = _____

WIOSPHR = _____

ATES = _____

BCRSIES = _____

AECHSR = _____

Color By Number
Use the color map below to color the picture

Color Map
1 = yellow
2 = orange
3 = light blue
4 = dark blue

Wise Men Give Gifts to Jesus

11 They came into the house and saw the young child with Mary, his mother, and they fell down and worshipped him. Opening their treasures, they offered to him gifts: gold, frankincense, and myrrh.
12 Being warned in a dream not to return to Herod, they went back to their own country another way.
Matthew 2:11-12 WEB

Wise Men Give Gifts to Jesus
Color the Picture

Spot the Difference
Spot 6 Differences Below and Circle Them

Wise Men Give Gifts to Jesus
Help the Wise Men Give Gifts to Jesus

Wise Men Give Gifts to Jesus

```
Z  F  P  Z  H  H  W  I  R  K  O  P  X  I  Z  C  T
C  P  R  R  G  K  F  Z  M  E  A  W  Z  H  E  U  B
W  P  W  A  R  N  E  D  K  N  K  P  O  W  J  X  L
B  M  Y  Q  N  R  L  E  G  I  V  U  D  L  O  G  U
I  Q  M  T  J  K  L  V  P  W  S  L  N  H  N  S  B
G  U  L  W  U  Y  I  W  K  E  I  W  T  L  T  L  M
O  A  K  R  O  H  F  N  M  H  D  H  B  F  E  Q  R
H  W  P  Z  G  Q  A  H  C  D  C  I  I  A  S  V  Z
S  C  G  S  M  X  X  F  F  E  O  G  Q  J  N  O  X
V  N  Z  H  M  Y  O  Z  V  P  N  B  Q  L  U  K  A
E  R  L  W  V  O  R  U  Q  P  H  S  Q  K  X  R  M
V  Z  L  N  Q  U  T  R  M  I  J  Z  E  F  M  Z  V
X  L  K  R  J  N  Y  H  H  H  T  A  M  A  J  X
R  X  Q  M  O  G  W  A  E  S  E  H  F  J  E  J  M
X  V  X  S  T  O  P  J  T  R  E  A  S  U  R  E  S
K  V  Y  D  L  O  G  C  O  O  D  D  M  E  D  Q  N
D  M  V  Y  U  M  T  D  F  W  P  V  U  C  T  K  R
```

HOUSE	YOUNG	CHILD
MOTHER	FELL	WORSHIPPED
TREASURES	GIFTS	GOLD
FRANKINCENSE	MYRRH	WARNED
DREAM	HEROD	

Wise Men Give Gifts to Jesus

Use the passage for Wise Men Give Gifts to Jesus to solve the crossword

ACROSS:

1. WHERE THE WISE MEN CAME INTO. MATT. 2:11

2. THE WISEMEN SAW THE YOUNG _____. MATT 2:11

3. WHO WAS JESUS WITH? MATT 2:11

4. THE WISE MEN FELL DOWN AND _____. MATT 2:11

5. WHAT THE WISE MEN OPENED. MATT 2:11

6. HOW WERE THE WISE MEN WARNED? MATT 2:12

DOWN:

7. WHAT THE WISE MEN OFFERED TO JESUS. MATT 2:11

8. ONE OF THE GIFTS OFFERED. MATT 2:11

9. ONE OF THE GIFTS OFFERED. MATT 2:11

10. ONE OF THE GIFTS OFFERED. MATT 2:11

11. WHO THE WISEMEN DIDN'T WANT TO RETURN TO. MATT 2:12

12. THE WISE MEN RETURNED TO THEIR OWN _____. MATT 2:12

Wise Men Give Gifts to Jesus
Word Scramble

Use the passage for Wise Men Give Gifts to Jesus to unscramble these words

PPERODHIWS   = _____

SUSTRERAE   = _____

DLOG   = _____

RYMRH   = _____

UNERTR   = _____

NPGNEOI   = _____

GFIST   = _____

EFNKRNCSENIA   = _____

NWARDE   = _____

YUCTONR   = _____

SECRET CODE

USE THE DECODER MAP BELOW
TO DECODE THE SECRET MESSAGE

—— —— ——   —— —— —— —— —— —— ——   —— —— —— —— —— —— ——
20 8 5   23 9 19 5 13 5 14   2 18 15 21 7 8 20

—— —— —— ——,   —— —— —— —— —— —— —— —— —— —— —— ——,
7 15 12 4   6 18 1 14 11 9 14 3   5 14 19 5

—— —— ——   —— —— —— —— ——   —— ——   —— —— —— —— ——
1 14 4   13 25 18 18 8   20 15   10 5 19 21 19

DECODER MAP

1=A	2=B	3=C	4=D	5=E	6=F
7=G	8=H	9=I	10=J	11=K	
12=L	13=M	14=N	15=O	16=P	
17=Q	18=R	19=S	20=T	21=U	
22=V	23=W	24=X	25=Y	26=Z	

Flight to Egypt

26 Now when they (Wise Men) had departed, behold, an angel of the Lord appeared to Joseph in a dream, saying, "Arise and take the young child and his mother, and flee into Egypt, and stay there until I tell you, for Herod will seek the young child to destroy him."

14 He arose and took the young child and his mother by night and departed into Egypt, 15 and was there until the death of Herod, that it might be fulfilled which was spoken by the Lord through the prophet, saying, "Out of Egypt I called my son." But when Herod was dead, behold, an angel of the Lord appeared in a dream to Joseph in Egypt, saying, 20 "Arise and take the young child and his mother and go into the land of Israel, for those who sought the young child's life are dead." 21 He arose and took the young child and his mother, and came into the land of Israel....22 Being warned in a dream, he withdrew into the region of Galilee, 23 and came and lived in a city called Nazareth; that it might be fulfilled which was spoken through the prophets that he (Jesus) will be called a Nazarene.

Matthew 2:13-15,19-23 WEB

Flight to Egypt

Color the Picture

Spot the Difference
Spot 6 Differences Below and Circle Them

Flight to Egypt
Find the Path to Egypt

Flight to Egypt

```
P D L U F F D Y S K C V P
F C E Y G S P Y F V K G A
Y V A P V I E O A J H A N
A C R W A I I R I K T Q X
G E S E V R I T Z G Z A V
L N I N Z S T S K X T D W
R E I R E H Y E S X Z R H
Q R E G W S F D D G S E Z
W A G L H U H L D E R A T
W Z Y D I T U E E O H M I
K A P P M L Q K D E S P L
N N T L O B A U E B Z F V
D Q F Z X F Q G T P X C I
```

DREAM	ARISE	FLEE
EGYPT	HEROD	SEEK
DESTROY	NIGHT	DEPARTED
ISRAEL	GALILEE	NAZARENE

Flight to Egypt

Use the passage for Flight to Egypt to solve the crossword

ACROSS:

1. _____ AND TAKE THE YOUNG CHILD... MATT 2:13

2. WHERE JOSEPH WAS TO FLEE TO. MATT 2:13

3. WHAT JOSEPH WAS TO DO WITH HIS FAMILY. MATT 2:13

4. _____ THERE UNTIL I TELL YOU. MATT 2:13

5. THEY STAYED IN EGYPT UNTIL THE _____ OF HEROD. MATT 2:15

6. AFTER HEROD DIED, WHERE JOSEPH WAS TO GO. MATT 2:21

DOWN:

7. WHO WAS A THREAT TO JESUS? MATT 2:13

8. WHAT HEROD WANTED TO DO TO JESUS. MATT 2:13

9. WHEN DID JOSEPH FLEE? MATT 2:14

10. JESUS WOULD BE CALLED A _____. MATT 2:23

Flight to Egypt
Word Scramble

Use the passage for Flight to Egypt to unscramble these words

IARES = _____

MHETRO = _____

TGPYE = _____

DYTREOS = _____

IDLELUFFL = _____

LHDCI = _____

LFEE = _____

HDREO = _____

LLGIEEA = _____

EZAANENR = _____

Color By Number

Color Map
1=dark brown   2= medium brown   3= light brown   4=dark pink   5=medium pink   6=blue   7=dark gray
8=medium gray   9=light gray   10=orange   11=medium yellow   12-light yellow   13= black   14=light pink

Spot the Difference
Spot 6 Differences Below and Circle Them

Adam and Eve's Sin

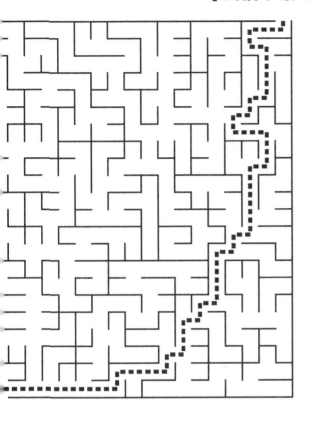

```
D W H N V H Z S Z D V A E T
E V R S W E L W B H K E W Q
C D E D N A M M O C X G J U
E P I W C D J S M A N L J N
I F W N X G T I B D E Y O F
V G B R U I S E E E A O N Z
E S N S L A Z Z H H T E W O
D P F I E F O T R E E E O I
F O T X R R S T A W N S M V
Q Y K U Z P P M T H T Z A V
R Q I P G F S E F A U M N R
K T E W H L B F N Y S G L K
Y K A Y M G M N F T P V L K
B N S S Y R Y G H O B T K J
```

YAHWEH	MAN	WOMAN
SERPENT	EATEN	COMMANDED
TREE	FRUIT	DECEIVED
HOSTILITY	BETWEEN	OFFSPRING
BRUISE	HEAD	HEEL

CROSS:

OD SAID, HAVE YOU _____ FROM THE TREE? GEN 3:11"
WHO THE HOSTILITY WILL BE BETWEEN. GEN 3:15
THAT EVE'S OFFSPRING WILL DO TO THE SERPENT'S HEAD. GEN 3:15
WHAT THE SERPENT WILL BRUISE ON EVE'S OFFSPRING. GEN 3:15

WN:
WHAT GOD WILL PUT BETWEEN THE SERPENT AND THE WOMAN. GEN

WHO EVE'S OFFSPRING REFERS TO...THINK BETHLEHEM. GEN 3:15
WHO ADAM BLAMED. GEN 3:12
WHO EVE BLAMED. GEN 3:13
THIS WAS ON THE TREE. GEN 3:12
WHAT THE SERPENT DID TO GET EVE TO EAT THE FRUIT. GEN 3:13

TNAEE	= EATEN
EMACMDDNO	= COMMANDED
UITFR	= FRUIT
TPNESER	= SERPENT
YHILTOSTI	= HOSTILITY
EETR	= TREE
WMAON	= WOMAN
ETA	= ATE
VCEEDEID	= DECEIVED
RIUBSE	= BRUISE

Spot the Difference
Spot 6 Differences Below and Circle Them

God's Promise to Abraham

```
P L H L I U V E K J L Z J T
Q U S Q A W B E Z M I W A A
Z C S G R F I B H I L F V H
E Z S N O I T A N W G V R C
X D S E F W P L T U I P R Z
E C S L V B M S A M Y Y B B
F Q E Z Y I E A E O K Q V H
S A L D B I T P R O H T E V
L H B E L V N A G B R V V W
U T N I E E O E L O A O E H
L R M I V U C A R E X S C J
R A Q P X K N R L E R L M S
F E L A Y D O Z G U U J D Q
Y H B L B I I C C S A J U O
```

ABRAM   LEAVE   RELATIVES
LAND   GREAT   NATION
BLESS   CURSE   CONTEMPT
ALL   FAMILIES   EARTH

Crossword

```
            7R            9B
5C U R S E      8G    L          10F
            L    R    E          A
         2L E A V E   S          M
            T    A    S          I
         6C  I    T   I    4N A T I O N
            O V       N          L
         3H O U S E   G          I
            N S                  E
            T                    S
       1A B R A M
            Y
```

CROSS:
ABRAHAM'S FIRST NAME. GEN 12:1
WHAT GOD TOLD ABRAM TO DO. GEN 12:1
THIRD THING ABRAM WAS TO LEAVE. GEN 12:1
ABRAM WOULD BE MADE A GREAT ____. GEN 12:2
GOD WILL DO THIS TO THOSE WHO TREAT WITH CONTEMPT. GEN 12:3

OWN:
FIRST THING ABRAM WAS TO LEAVE. GEN 12:1
SECOND THING ABRAM WAS TO LEAVE. GEN 12:1
GOD WILL MAKE ABRAM'S NAME _____. GEN 12:2
ABRAM WILL BE THIS. GEN 12:2
. WHO WILL BE BLESSED THROUGH ABRAM. GEN 12:3

Unscramble

BARAM   = ABRAM

EAEILSVRT   = RELATIVES

AGTER   = GREAT

LSSBE   = BLESS

IFLIASME   = FAMILIES

AELEV   = LEAVE

DLNA   = LAND

ONNTAI   = NATION

SCEUR   = CURSE

ATRHE   = EARTH

Spot the Difference
Spot 6 Differences Below and Circle Them

The Angel Tells Mary Jesus Will Be Born To Her

```
Y F A K S U L P W P L M M
P G S S A L V J D T F F W
U A A W N D X W Y R A M N
N B O F G V E O Q M S S O
L R A S E E I R K X E K B
D I J D L L R R O J R R S
F E O I E D B I G V V I H
P L L Q L S F K T I A A P
E A A B J E S U S Z N F E
G F L G U M S E A O T Y S
F O Z I S O Z H L V S J O
E M X D J T R F X B X W J
A N A Z A R E T H T N O M
```

MONTH	GABRIEL	GALILEE
NAZARETH	VIRGIN	JOSEPH
MARY	ANGEL	FAVORED
BLESSED	TROUBLED	JESUS
SERVANT	WORD	

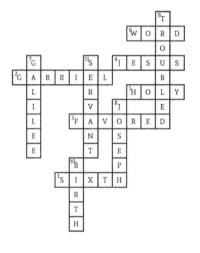

SS:

E MONTH THE ANGEL CAME TO MARY. LUKE 1:26

ME OF THE ANGEL. LUKE 1:26

OICE, YOU HIGHLY _____ ONE. LUKE 1:28

E NAME MARY WOULD GIVE TO HER SON. LUKE 1:31

E _____ SPIRIT WOULD OVERSHADOW MARY. LUKE 1:35

IT BE DONE ACCORDING TO GOD'S _____. LUKE 1:38

N:

E CITY WHERE MARY LIVED. LUKE 1:26

E MAN MARY WAS PLEDGED TO BE MARRIED TO. LUKE 1:27

AT MARY WAS WHEN THE ANGEL GREETED HER. LUKE 1:29

ARY WOULD GIVE _____ TO A SON. LUKE 1:31

ARY DESCRIBES HERSELF AS THIS. LUKE 1:38

XHIST	= SIXTH
IEGLELA	= GALILEE
RIDAMER	= MARRIED
CEOJREI	= REJOICE
ETLORDBU	= TROUBLED
MNTHO	= MONTH
NIVGRI	= VIRGIN
ENLAG	= ANGEL
EFDRVAO	= FAVORED
NRSTVEA	= SERVANT

Spot the Difference
Spot 6 Differences Below and Circle Them

NO ROOM!

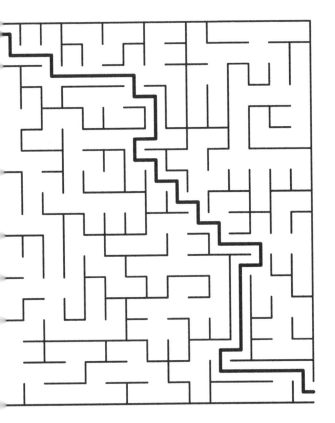

G	G	O	I	S	P	C	H	X	S	X	Z	Y	W
T	H	T	R	O	U	G	H	U	K	Z	V	L	O
Z	B	F	A	O	M	I	N	N	K	G	Y	P	U
A	E	I	F	L	N	V	N	R	J	S	P	I	R
D	T	Q	X	G	B	A	V	I	A	O	J	F	K
U	H	R	R	I	G	J	Z	R	R	S	P	X	Y
P	L	W	R	K	V	A	F	A	C	I	E	X	T
N	E	T	P	W	V	Q	L	Q	R	N	U	A	I
V	H	J	O	R	J	M	F	I	R	E	B	Q	C
S	E	P	O	A	W	M	B	O	L	A	T	Z	L
O	M	O	Z	P	E	L	L	M	G	E	T	H	O
V	M	F	M	P	T	L	E	E	R	C	E	D	T
W	M	H	R	E	E	M	Z	I	L	E	Z	R	H
Q	Q	E	G	D	X	S	I	W	W	P	C	C	S

DECREE	CAESAR	ENROLLED
QUIRINIUS	CITY	GALILEE
NAZARETH	BETHLEHEM	BIRTH
WRAPPED	CLOTHS	TROUGH
ROOM	INN	

CROSS:
5. EVERYONE WENT TO HIS OWN _____ TO ENROLL. LUKE 2:3
4. WHERE DAVID WENT TO ENROLL. LUKE 2:4
3. JOSEPH WAS OF THE FAMILY OF THIS PERSON. LUKE 2:4
4. WHAT MARY DID WITH JESUS. LUKE 2:7
1. WHERE MARY LAID JESUS. LUKE 2:6

DOWN:
6. WHAT WENT OUT FROM CAESAR. LUKE 2:1
7. ALL OF THIS SHOULD BE ENROLLED. LUKE 2:1
8. WHO WAS GOVERNOR OF SYRIA. LUKE 2:2
9. MARY'S CONDITION AT THIS TIME. LUKE 2:5
10. JESUS WAS MARY'S _____ SON. LUKE 2:6

CDREEE	= DECREE
HMBEELTHE	= BETHLEHEM
IRHBT	= BIRTH
APPDRWE	= WRAPPED
HUOGRT	= TROUGH
DORLELEN	= ENROLLED
NGPENRAT	= PREGNANT
NFTRSBIRO	= FIRSTBORN
TLHCO	= CLOTH
RMOO	= ROOM

Crossword answers:
- 5. TROUGH
- 4. WRAPPED
- 1. CITY
- 2. BETHLEHEM
- 3. DAVID
- 6. DECREE
- 7. WORLD
- 8. QUIRINIUS
- 9. PREGNANT
- 10. FIRSTBORN

Spot the Difference
Spot 6 Differences Below and Circle Them

The Angel Tells Shepherds About Jesus' Birth

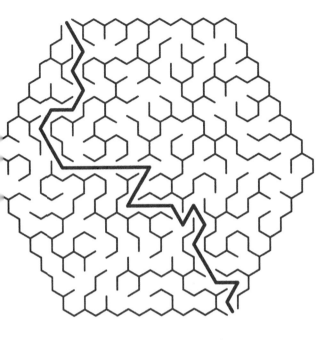

```
P  F  R  D  Q  I  D  B  U  I  E  X  N  J
D  V  E  V  K  P  P  I  X  Y  C  K  R  B
Q  I  B  R  O  I  V  A  S  B  A  B  Y  N
Y  X  A  J  L  D  A  K  P  M  E  B  M  A
H  P  H  R  U  Z  X  V  Y  K  P  X  R  J
S  T  S  H  F  N  G  I  S  S  C  L  A  Q
Y  D  E  P  P  A  R  W  G  T  S  O  Q  Y
R  R  K  R  G  S  J  K  W  W  Q  V  L  D
V  Z  O  Y  R  C  N  U  C  T  N  N  T  F
H  J  O  L  F  I  E  L  D  L  E  G  N  A
A  J  T  U  G  N  F  R  U  V  O  O  F  T
K  D  R  H  E  J  R  I  A  U  T  O  X  B
K  U  T  W  Y  D  N  E  E  U  K  D  B  I
E  M  S  H  E  P  H  E  R  D  S  X  D  N
```

SHEPHERDS	FIELD	FLOCK
NIGHT	ANGEL	GLORY
TERRIFIED	AFRAID	GOOD
NEWS	JOY	SAVIOR
SIGN	BABY	WRAPPED
HEAVENLY	ARMY	PEACE

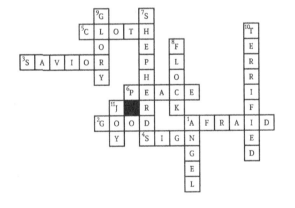

Crossword:
```
        9G      7S
    5C  L  O  T  H
        O     H         10T
3S  A  V  I  O  R        E
        R     H   8F     R
              P   L      R
           6P  E  A  C  E   I
        11J    R  O        F
      2G  O  O  D      1A  F  R  A  I  D
        Y     4S  I  G  N   E
                       G    D
                       E
                       L
```

OSS:
HE ANGEL TOLD THEM NOT TO BE _____. LUKE 2:10
HAT KIND OF NEWS DID THE ANGEL BRING? LUKE 2:10
HO WAS BORN UNTO THEM THAT DAY? LUKE 2:11
HIS IS A _____ TO YOU. LUKE 2:12
HE BABY WOULD BE WRAPPED IN STRIPS OF _____. LUKE 2:12
LORY TO GOD AND ON EARTH _____. LUKE 2:14

'N:
HO CAME TO SEE THE SHEPHERDS. LUKE 2:9
HO WAS IN A FIELD. LUKE 2:8
HAT THE SHEPHERDS WERE WATCHING OVER. LUKE 2:8
HE _____ OF THE LORD SHONE AROUND THEM. LUKE 2:9
OW THE SHEPHERDS FELT WHEN THEY SAW THE ANGEL. LUKE 2:9
HE NEWS WAS OF GREAT _____. LUKE 2:10

EEHSRPDHS	= SHEPHERDS
WCHTA	= WATCH
GRLOY	= GLORY
SWNE	= NEWS
SNIG	= SIGN
DLFEI	= FIELD
COLKF	= FLOCK
DEEIRTIRF	= TERRIFIED
JYO	= JOY
LTTIMUDUE	= MULTITUDE

Spot the Difference
Spot 6 Differences Below and Circle Them

Jesus is Born

```
Z H B S J J Z K V Z G W S J
V T X E P O F R H X E Y B I
E L R D B S U T Y V N C M W
J J Y I J E D N S R G M M W
P T V E G P C A F R A I D P
H L S S S H V N D N G M S W
B U Y D O E T G U Y E A C V
S E K N N T C E S B D W Q C
T N O R H A L R O P U G D Y
G Z I F U N F P E U W T R X
Q X J S T G J D A T S X R K
A N G O M E X A M P L E G C
U Q A V A L S I V T K Y H U
Z I V I B B I R T H V O F I
```

ENGAGED   PREGNANT   MARY
JOSEPH   RIGHTEOUS   EXAMPLE
SECRETLY   ANGEL   AFRAID
BIRTH   SON   JESUS
SAVE   SINS   IMMANUEL

AYMR = MARY
SUDHNAB = HUSBAND
LPIUBC = PUBLIC
ETLECSYR = SECRETLY
AVES = SAVE
HPJOSE = JOSEPH
RGHOETUSI = RIGHTEOUS
LEXMAEP = EXAMPLE
DAMER = DREAM
DAEPDETR = DEPARTED

CROSS:

1 MARY WAS _____ TO JOSEPH. MATT 1:18
2 JOSEPH DIDN'T WANT TO MAKE MARY A PUBLIC _____. MATT 1:19
3 THE ANGEL APPEARED TO JOSEPH IN A _____. MATT 1:20
4 WHAT JESUS WOULD DO FOR HIS PEOPLE. MATT 1:21
5 ALL THIS HAPPENED SO THAT IT MIGHT BE _____. MATT 1:22
6 IMMANUEL MEANS GOD _____ US. MATT 1:23

DOWN:

7 MARY'S HUSBAND. MATT 1:19
8 THE KIND OF MAN JOSEPH WAS. MATT 1:19
9 HOW JOSEPH WAS GOING TO PUT MARY AWAY. MATT 1:19
10 WHO CAME TO JOSEPH. MATT 1:20
11 THE ANGEL TOLD JOSEPH NOT TO BE _____. MATT 1:20
12 WHO DID THE LORD SPEAK A PROPHECY THROUGH. MATT 1:22
13 THEY SHALL CALL HIS NAME _____. MATT 1:23

Spot the Difference
Spot 6 Differences Below and Circle Them

Wise Men See the Star

```
R E B E T H L E H E M V N R
L A Y O J X C D H B W C S K
K A T J N H M O U U B Z B S
O W I S E M E N B H D E A T
Z M S Q H S L R C E A Y L S
Y X B Q M R A O L R W O M I
U L K X M E S B S O O H C B
H N T Q J J U H J D R N R F
K V T E O O R K N W S G L C
O P S S R I E X V C H S X V
Q D A T E C J T R U I L Q H
L H E Q Y E E Z X I P T A F
V S T O O D I S V K W I N D
S L T D L N M M M I O H V M
```

HEROD	WISEMEN	EAST
STAR	WORSHIP	TROUBLED
JERUSALEM	BORN	BETHLEHEM
SECRETLY	STOOD	REJOICED
JOY		

Crossword (filled): TROUBLED, WISEMEN, HEROD, WORSHIP, KING, SECRETLY, STAR, BETHLEHEM, REJOICED, DILIGENTLY

SEMNEIW	= WISEMEN
KNGI	= KING
OERBDTLU	= TROUBLED
JCIEODRE	= REJOICED
EYRCLTSE	= SECRETLY
RLSJEEAUM	= JERUSALEM
WIOSPHR	= WORSHIP
ATES	= EAST
BCRSIES	= SCRIBES
AECHSR	= SEARCH

CROSS:

...HO WAS KING WHEN JESUS WAS BORN. MATT 2:1
...IESE CAME FROM THE EAST. MATT 2:1
...SUS WAS CONSIDERED THE _____ OF THE JEWS. MATT 2:2
...OW HEROD CALLED THE WISE MEN. MATT 2:7
...HAT HEROD SAID HE WOULD DO WHEN THEY FOUND JESUS. MATT 2:8

...WN:

...HERE JESUS WAS BORN. MATT. 2:1
...IIS WAS SEEN IN THE EAST. MATT 2:2
...NG HEROD WAS _____ WHEN HE HEARD IT. MATT 2:3
...) AND SEARCH _____ FOR THE YOUNG CHILD. MATT 2:8
...VHAT THE WISEMEN DID WHEN THEY SAW THE STAR. MATT 2:10

Spot the Difference
Spot 6 Differences Below and Circle Them

Wise Men Give Gifts to Jesus

```
Z  F  P  Z  H  H  W  I  R  K  O  P  X  I  Z  C  T
C  P  R  R  G  K  F  Z  M  E  A  W  Z  H  E  U  B
W  P  W  A  R  N  E  D  K  N  K  P  O  W  J  X  L
B  M  Y  Q  N  R  L  E  G  I  V  U  D  L  O  G  U
I  Q  M  T  J  K  L  V  P  W  S  L  N  H  N  S  B
G  U  L  W  U  Y  I  W  K  E  I  W  T  L  T  L  M
O  A  K  R  O  H  F  N  M  H  D  H  B  F  E  Q  R
H  W  P  Z  G  Q  A  H  C  D  C  I  I  A  S  V  Z
S  C  G  S  M  X  X  F  E  O  G  Q  J  N  O  X
V  N  Z  H  M  Y  O  Z  V  P  N  B  Q  L  U  K  A
E  R  L  W  V  O  R  U  Q  P  H  S  Q  K  X  R  M
V  Z  L  N  Q  U  T  R  M  I  J  Z  E  F  M  Z  V
X  L  K  R  J  N  Y  H  H  H  T  H  A  M  A  J  X
R  X  Q  M  O  G  W  A  E  S  E  H  F  J  E  M
X  V  X  S  T  O  P  J  T  R  E  A  S  U  R  E  S
K  V  Y  D  L  O  G  C  O  O  D  D  M  E  D  Q  N
D  M  V  Y  U  M  T  D  F  W  P  V  U  C  T  K  R
```

HOUSE	YOUNG	CHILD
MOTHER	FELL	WORSHIPPED
TREASURES	GIFTS	GOLD
FRANKINCENSE	MYRRH	WARNED
DREAM	HEROD	

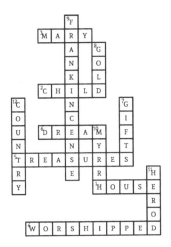

CROSS:
WHERE THE WISE MEN CAME INTO. MATT. 2:11
THE WISEMEN SAW THE YOUNG _____. MATT 2:11
WHO WAS JESUS WITH? MATT 2:11
THE WISE MEN FELL DOWN AND _____. MATT 2:11
WHAT THE WISE MEN OPENED. MATT 2:11
HOW WERE THE WISE MEN WARNED? MATT 2:12

DOWN:
WHAT THE WISE MEN OFFERED TO JESUS. MATT 2:11
ONE OF THE GIFTS OFFERED. MATT 2:11
ONE OF THE GIFTS OFFERED. MATT 2:11
ONE OF THE GIFTS OFFERED. MATT 2:11
WHO THE WISEMEN DIDN'T WANT TO RETURN TO. MATT 2:12
THE WISE MEN RETURNED TO THEIR OWN _____. MATT 2:12

PPERODHIWS	= WORSHIPPED
SUSTRERAE	= TREASURES
DLOG	= GOLD
RYMRH	= MYRRH
UNERTR	= RETURN
NPGNEOI	= OPENING
GFIST	= GIFTS
EFNKRNCSENIA	= FRANKINCENSE
NWARDE	= WARNED
YUCTONR	= COUNTRY

Spot the Difference
Spot 6 Differences Below and Circle Them

Flight to Egypt

```
P D L U F F D Y S K C V P
F C E Y G S P Y F V K G A
Y V A P V I E O A J H A N
A C R W A I I R I K T Q X
G E S E V R I T Z G Z A V
L N I N Z S T S K X T D W
R E I R E H Y E S X Z R H
Q R E G W S F D D G S E Z
W A G L H U H L D E R A T
W Z Y D I T U E E O H M I
K A P P M L Q K D E S P L
N N T L O B A U E B Z F V
D Q F Z X F Q G T P X C I
```

DREAM   ARISE   FLEE
EGYPT   HEROD   SEEK
DESTROY   NIGHT   DEPARTED
ISRAEL   GALILEE   NAZARENE

```
        8D
        E       7H
  6I S R A E L       9N
        T   R       I
        R   O  10N  G
        O    5D E A T H
2E G Y P T      Z   T
          4S T A Y
            R
          3F L E E
            N
        1A R I S E
```

CROSS:

1 ____ AND TAKE THE YOUNG CHILD... MATT 2:13
2 WHERE JOSEPH WAS TO FLEE TO. MATT 2:13
3 WHAT JOSEPH WAS TO DO WITH HIS FAMILY. MATT 2:13
4 _____ THERE UNTIL I TELL YOU. MATT 2:13
5 THEY STAYED IN EGYPT UNTIL THE ____ OF HEROD. MATT 2:15
6 AFTER HEROD DIED, WHERE JOSEPH WAS TO GO. MATT 2:21

DOWN:

7 WHO WAS A THREAT TO JESUS? MATT 2:13
8 WHAT HEROD WANTED TO DO TO JESUS. MATT 2:13
9 WHEN DID JOSEPH FLEE? MATT 2:14
10 JESUS WOULD BE CALLED A _____. MATT 2:23

IARES	= ARISE
MHETRO	= MOTHER
TGPYE	= EGYPT
DYTREOS	= DESTROY
IDLELUFFL	= FULFILLED
LHDCI	= CHILD
LFEE	= FLEE
HDREO	= HEROD
LLGIEEA	= GALILEE
EZAANENR	= NAZARENE

Bonus Puzzle!!

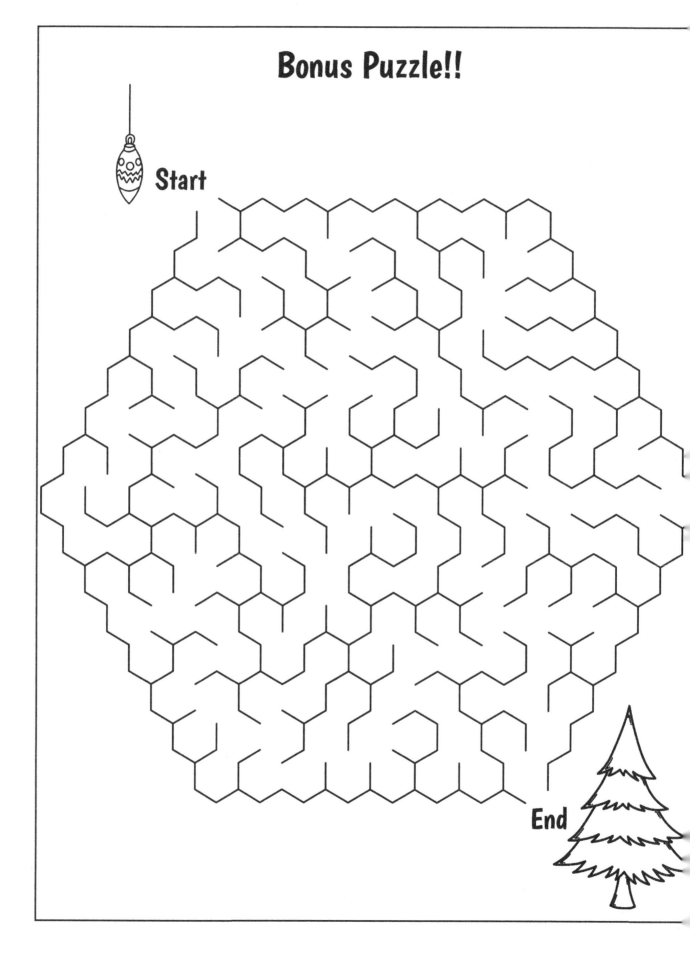

Start

End

Made in the USA
Las Vegas, NV
30 November 2024

13003566R00057